THE VIOLENT EARTH
VOLCANO

John Dudman

Wayland

Titles in this series

Earthquake
Flood
Storm
Volcano

Editor: Sarah Doughty
Designer: Tony Truscott
Artist: Nick Hawken
Consultant: Sandy Lawson,
engineering seismologist

First published in 1992 by
Wayland (Publishers) Ltd
61 Western Road, Hove
East Sussex, BN3 1JD, England

**British Library Cataloguing in
Publication Data**
Dudman, John
   Volcano. – (The violent earth)
   I. Title II. Series
   551.21

ISBN 0 7502 0365 X

Typeset by Tony Truscott Designs
Printed in Italy by Rotolito Lombarda
S.p.A.
Bound in France by A.G.M.

Picture: A river of red-hot lava pours from the
glowing peak of a volcano.

CONTENTS

THE FIRE MOUNTAIN EXPLODES

To everyone in Washington State on the Pacific coast of the USA, Mount St Helens is the 'Fire Mountain', the name given to it by native Americans living in the surrounding Cascade Mountains. Five times in 280 years, the smoking peak of the 'Fire Mountain' has exploded.

Prediction

In the 1970s, scientists predicted that another eruption was near. But years passed as they studied the build-up to the next major eruption. It was the most closely recorded watch on volcanic activity in modern history. After sleeping for over 120 years, the volcano awoke in March 1980. During the next two months, the earth on its north face bulged into a 'blister'

Big New Rain of Ash

VOLCANO BLOWS AGAIN

San Francisco Chronicle
The Largest Daily Circulation in Northern California

116th Year No. 128   ★ ★ ★ ★   FRIDAY, JUNE 13, 1980   777-1111   20 CENTS

Tortured Terrain

Clouds of Ash Fall Over Cities

1.6 km wide, as molten rock bubbled towards the surface. The summit's cone slowly opened wider and wider.

State emergency systems sounded the alarm as scientists noted every sound and shudder that came from Mount St Helens. One thousand Americans were evacuated from a zone 32 km around the smouldering volcano. Harry Truman, 84, owner of Mount Helens Lodge close to the smoking cone, refused to leave. 'If the mountain goes, I'm going to stay right here,' he said. 'I stuck it out for 54 years and I can stick it out now.' His body was never found.

The explosion

At 8.32 am on 18 May, the volcano blasted out of the north face of the mountain. People living 16 km away were tossed from their beds. For nine hours Mount St Helens fumed.

Left: This is the scenic view of Mount St Helens before it exploded.

'I stopped and looked and saw a boiling mass of cloud pursuing me. The cloud was like a wall about three miles across, extending straight up... it was very dramatic.' (Keith Ronnholm).

A billowing cloud of smoke and ash rose 25 km into the sky when Mount St Helens erupted.

Forest devastated

Mud flows in rivers

Area devastated

Ash cloud

Mount St Helens

NORTH AMERICA

Mount St Helens

0   10 km

Left: When Mount St Helens blew up, an area 30 km wide was devastated in minutes.

Below: This aerial photograph shows the crater that was formed when the peak of Mount St Helens was blown off.

Ash and charred trees covered the ground in the area near to where the volcano erupted.

Molten rocks were thrown high into the sky. An avalanche of red hot lava and sizzling mud poured down its sides, and a towering black cloud of ash was caught by strong winds to be carried south and east, falling on towns in Idaho and Montana. Roads became so thick with grey ash in some places that snowploughs were needed to clear them. The dust choked car engines into silence in four states. In 17 days, the volcano's dust and ash circled the world.

Land is reshaped
Despite the early warnings, 57 people were killed and two million animals – deer, elks, bears and birds – died as pine forests were set alight. Once green meadows and lush forests were turned into bubbling seas

> *'Huge old growth fir trees were flattened like a million wooden matches... everywhere was grey-white ash...and mud of countless shades of brown and grey.' (by the Associated Press).*

of black volcanic rock and mud. Today, the foothills are dotted with colourful wild flowers and young pine, alder and aspen trees grow. Every year, nearly two million tourists visit the hillsides to see how nature changed the face of the 'Fire Mountain' and then helped it to heal its wounds.

Scientists hope that the scientific data provided before the explosion and after it happened will help them to understand more about how volcanoes are born and how they behave.

7

UNDERNEATH A VOLCANO

Inside the earth

The planet that we live on is made up of three layers. Deep inside the earth is the fiery core, where the temperature is thought to be over 2,500 °C. The inner core is made up of solid material while the outer core is thought to be liquid.

Above the core lies the mantle, which is solid rock but is still very hot. The mantle supports the earth's enormous tectonic plates. These plates are the size of continents. They stand next to each other but are constantly moving because they are under pressure from the earth's centre.

A section through the earth, showing the crust, the mantle and the core.

A Cross-Section of the Earth

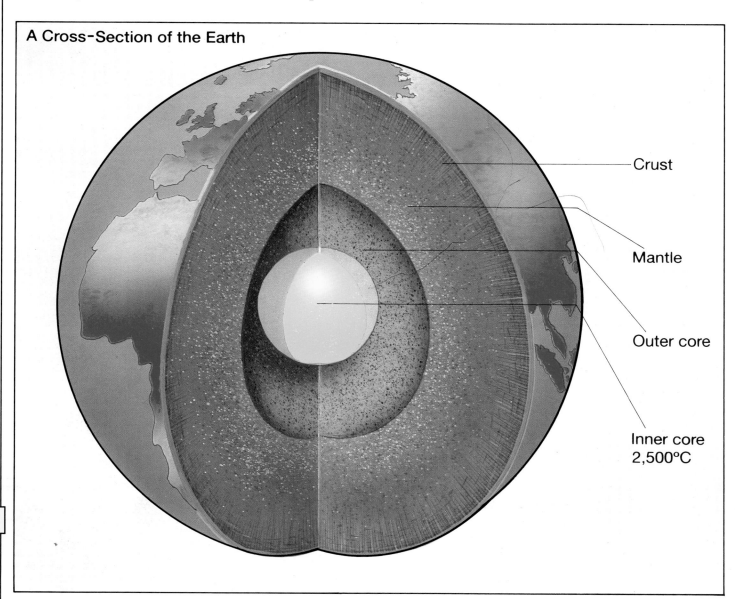

Crust

Mantle

Outer core

Inner core
2,500°C

The plates make up part of the earth's crust and mantle.

Magma

When volcanoes erupt, the material that rises out of a volcano is called magma – a mixture of molten rock and gas. The magma is formed in the lower part of the crust and the upper part of the mantle. This is because the rocks are hot enough for a small amount of magma to melt.

If enough magma is formed, it begins to rise up to the surface through cracks in the rocks in the earth's crust. The heat explodes through the ground, blasting fizzing rocks into the air and spilling lava in all directions as a volcanic eruption.

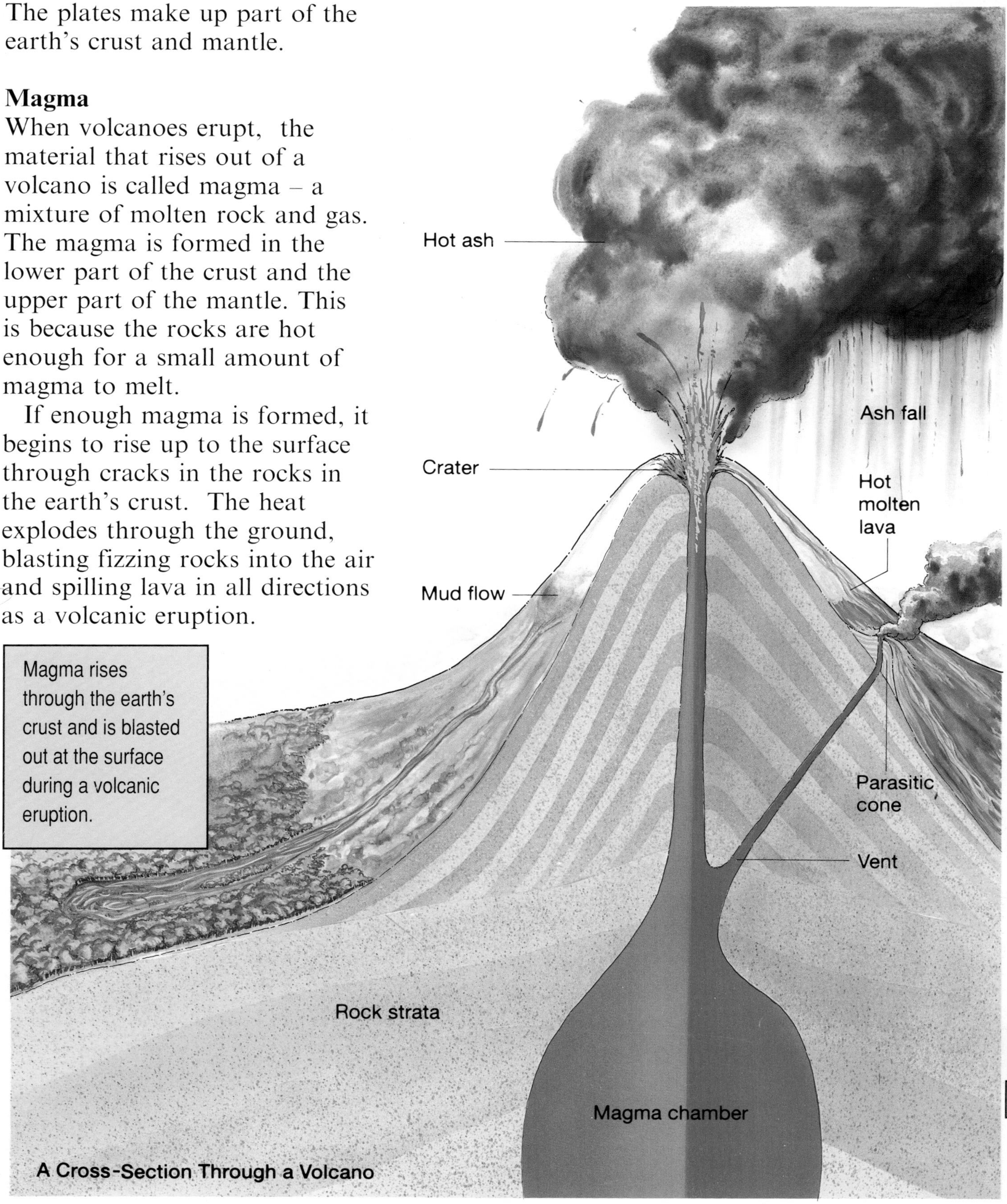

Magma rises through the earth's crust and is blasted out at the surface during a volcanic eruption.

Hot ash

Ash fall

Crater

Hot molten lava

Mud flow

Parasitic cone

Vent

Rock strata

Magma chamber

A Cross-Section Through a Volcano

Volcanoes usually occur in places where the earth's plates meet, and magma rises from underground.

Countries that are on the edge of the Pacific Ocean are particularly at risk. They stand above the 'Ring of Fire', which is a string of volcanoes formed where plates join in the Far East. The volcanoes follow a line of weakness from the Americas over the Aleutian Range (south of the Bering Sea) down to Japan and the Philippines, and on to Indonesia and New Zealand.

Plate edges

Volcanic activity occurs along these plate edges when the underground plates grind together. Magma rises from the mantle as the path to the surface is easiest at the plate boundaries.

Hot spots

Other volcanoes can also occur but are not found near plate edges. They are found in places known as 'hot spots' where the crust of the earth is very thin and molten rock can easily force its way through and collect in a magma chamber inside the volcano. Eventually the pressure becomes so great that the volcano erupts.

Types of volcano

As volcanoes erupt, lava and ash are built up into a hill or mountain, called the cone of the volcano. Some volcanoes form with very gently sloping sides, caused by fluid lava which flows a long way before it cools. Other volcanoes have a sticky lava which quickly builds up a steep sided volcano of ash and cinder.

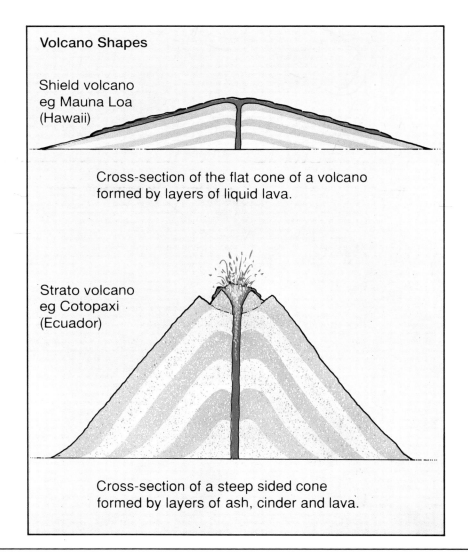

Volcano Shapes

Shield volcano
eg Mauna Loa
(Hawaii)

Cross-section of the flat cone of a volcano formed by layers of liquid lava.

Strato volcano
eg Cotopaxi
(Ecuador)

Cross-section of a steep sided cone formed by layers of ash, cinder and lava.

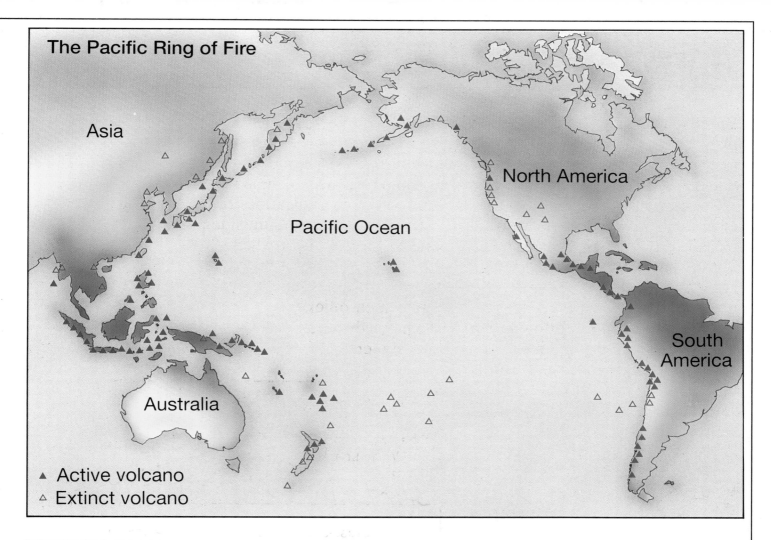

The Pacific Ring of Fire

Asia

North America

Pacific Ocean

South America

Australia

▲ Active volcano
△ Extinct volcano

Above: Many explosive volcanoes occur where plates collide along the Pacific Ring of Fire.

Left: Parícutin is a recently-formed volcano in Mexico, which lies along the Pacific Ring of Fire.

ISLANDS BORN IN THE SEA

At least eighty active volcanoes are known to be on the ocean sea-beds. Sometimes when they erupt their cones burst above the sea to create islands. The most dramatic example happened during the night of 14-15 November 1963 off the south coast of Iceland, which is a huge volcanic island on the edge of the Arctic Circle in the North Atlantic.

The birth of the island of Surtsey in November, 1963.

Underwater activity

The first signs of activity under the water were huge bubbles bursting through the waves from the sea-bed 200 m below. Then the smouldering lava appeared, followed by ballooning smoke and ash that rose in a grey column several thousands of metres into the sky.

The island takes shape

Ships and aircraft were warned to keep clear of the area in case an explosion occurred. Icelanders, however, queued in the capital of Reykjavik to take flights over the boiling sea where the island slowly took shape before their eyes. They named it Surtsey after a fire-god worshipped by their ancestors in olden days – Surtur.

Surtsey grows

Surtsey grew to over 2 sq km in size with a height of 170 m. Inside Surtsey's main cone, lava could be seen glowing from a deep basin. Around the peak five other smaller craters were created. Since its formation vegetation has sprouted amid the lava, and the new island has become a home for six species of birds and many insects.

'When darkness fell it was a pillar of fire and the entire cone was aglow with bombs which rolled down the slopes into the white surf around the island. Flashes of lightning lit up the eruption cloud and peals of thunder cracked above our heads.' (Sigurdur Thorainsson, Icelandic geologist).

Formation of Surtsey

1. The magma pushes up through the sea floor to make a new underwater volcano.

2. The lava erupts, mixes with the seawater and the lava flow forms a new island.

3. The lava cools under the sea and the island grows rapidly.

Island of Krakatoa

One of the biggest explosions in recorded history happened on 27 August 1883 when Krakatoa, one of a group of uninhabited Indonesian islands in the Sundra Strait, blew up violently. The noise was so loud that it awakened Australians 3,000 km away and rumbled 4,800 km across the Indian Ocean to Rodrigues Island off Mauritius.

A series of powerful explosions had rocked the volcanic islands all through the previous summer. But it was not until 26 August that Krakatoa became violently active.

Island splits in two

Every few minutes thunderous booms were heard together with a loud roar that continued until mid-morning the next day. Krakatoa was then blown in half by a blast that caused tsunamis 38 m high. The waves crashed on to the coasts of Sumatra and Java, sweeping away 36,000 people.

Tonnes of rock was thrown high into the air. For weeks, large chunks of rock known as volcanic bombs, fell into the Indian Ocean and South Seas, often splashing down close to ships.

Below left: This engraving of the eruption of Krakatoa in 1883 was based on a photograph taken shortly after the explosion had occurred.

Volcanic Activity on Krakatoa

1. Before 1883. The island of Krakatoa was formed by a group of volcanic cones.

Shock waves reach Britain

Shock waves from Krakatoa spread around the world. Sea levels rose along the western coast of the Americas. Even in the English Channel unusually high tides swept the English and French coasts. Krakatoa spluttered on angrily for nearly two days as its dust cloud, 80 km high circled the world, producing brilliant sunsets across the Far East, the USA and even in Britain.

'At 11.15 am on 27 August, there was a fearful explosion in the direction of Krakatoa. We saw a wave rush right on to Button Island, apparently sweeping right over the the south part. This we saw repeated twice. The same waves seemed also to run right on to the Java shore.

By 11.30 am we were enclosed in a darkness that might also be felt. We had to grope about the decks, and although speaking to each other, could not see each other.

This horrible state and downpour of mud continued until 1.30 pm, the roarings of the volcano and lightnings being something fearful.' (From the captain's log, on the British ship Charles Bal, off the coast of Java).

Pacific Ocean

Indian / Ocean

Krakatoa

Area explosion heard

Ash fall

0   3000km

AUSTRALIA

2. After 1883. Volcanic explosion destroyed most of the island and left a crater in the sea bed.

3. After 1927. Volcanic activity early this century formed a new island in the crater.

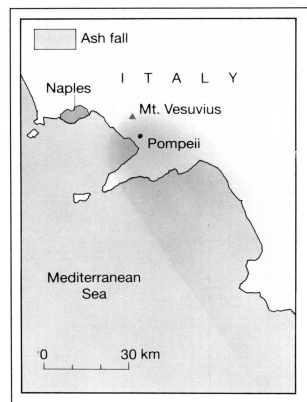

Ash fall

I T A L Y

Naples

Mt. Vesuvius

Pompeii

Mediterranean
Sea

0   30 km

Historic Eruptions

Date	Place	Result
1450 BC	Santorini, Greece	Destroyed
79 AD	Mt Vesuvius, Italy	20,000 dead
1669	Mt Etna, Sicily	20,000 dead
1586	Kelud, Java	10,000 dead
1792	Mt Unzen, Japan	15,000 dead
1815	Tambori, Indonesia	90,000 dead
1883	Krakatoa, Indonesia	36,000 dead

The death of Pompeii

The Krakatoan explosion was only one of many volcanic disasters through the ages. When Mount Vesuvius erupted on 24 August AD 79, it completely buried the city of Pompeii on the Gulf of Naples in ash 18 m deep, killing 20,000 Romans. Their bodies, homes and belongings were preserved to provide the nineteenth and twentieth centuries with a remarkable picture of life in Roman times.

Only a quarter of the people escaped the ash that fell from Vesuvius. Most of the dead were buried alive, poisoned by the phosphorus fumes from the ash that poured into their homes and swamped the streets and squares.

Right: The ruined city of Pompeii, once totally covered by a blanket of ash from Mount Vesuvius, is now visited by thousands of tourists every year.

Below: The body of a Pompeii victim cast by the hot ash that fell on Mount Vesuvius when it erupted in AD 79, killing 20,000 people.

Discovery of a hidden city

Fifteen hundred years later, labourers building an aqueduct found coins, rings, bracelets and part of a wall – clues to the hidden ruins. Excavations in the eighteenth century discovered much more. An underground city began to take shape, but it was not until 1861 that serious archaeological work began.

Since then, Pompeii has become a place of great historical interest. Plaster casts were taken of the cavities left by decomposing bodies. These show the position of the victims when they died. In houses, cooking utensils were found, in buildings mosaics and wall murals were discovered. In town squares handsome fountains were uncovered.

Mount Vesuvius last exploded in 1944, but the tremors and smoke that drifts from its crater show that the volcano is still very much alive.

Ancient history has recorded many volcanic disasters, but modern times have also had their own list of tragedies which have caused huge numbers of deaths.

Mont Pelée

In 1902 when Mont Pelée exploded on the Caribbean island of Martinique, it completely destroyed the town of St Pierre that lay 6 km from the volcano. A glowing avalanche of hot rock, gas and ash burst from the side of the volcano, which, within two minutes spread all over the town. There was only one survivor among 28,000 people.

He was a prisoner serving a jail sentence who was well protected in a thick-walled cell deep within

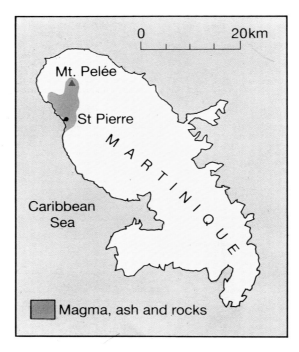

Magma, ash and rocks

Under this enormous cloud of smoke, an avalanche of fiery lava and ash swept down the side of Mont Pelée, and destroyed the town of St Pierre.

18

roars threw a mushroom cloud of ash 16 km above the volcano. Molten lava burst over its sides. As ash covered the countryside, many buildings collapsed under its weight. More than 200,000 refugees streamed from the volcano as their villages were buried. About 400 people died.

While Pinatubo raged, earthquakes shook Manila. A typhoon with vivid lightning swept the disaster area, turning mounds of ash into mud flows that poured down the mountainside at nearly 100 kph. As the wind rose, rocks the size of tennis balls hit villages 56 km away. Ash clouds turned noon into midnight.

Ash cloaks South-east Asia

In Ologapo, a town 40 km from Pinatubo, children played in streets covered deep in grey ash. The dust cloud fell 2,400 km away in Singapore, across Malaysia and over Vietnam, cloaking towns, rice fields and lakes. Pinatubo was still exploding a month after its first eruption, but the number killed was remarkably light for such strong volcanic activity.

Survivors tread carefully along ash-covered streets after Mount Pinatubo erupted in 1991, after 600 years asleep.

PREDICTING VOLCANOES

At any time about 20 volcanoes are erupting in the world. Scientists are now able to predict volcanic explosions much more accurately, even if they cannot tell the exact moment that they will happen. This usually allows enough time for people to be evacuated from an area.

There is no clear set of signs that tell us when a volcano will erupt. Volcanoes all behave in different ways. Sometimes they look as if they are about to explode. The smoke above active volcanoes like Mount Etna in Sicily, Vesuvius in Italy, and others in Hawaii and Alaska, thickens. The land shudders from deep tremors, vents appear on mountainsides to allow gathering gases to escape, cones widen, sometimes falling into the fuming crater. But sometimes the growing signals from a volcano just fade away.

At other times, a volcano, dormant for hundreds of years, awakes with little warning of its hidden power.

People examining the amount of damage caused to vineyards caught in a lava flow from Mount Etna in 1971.

Scientific methods

One way to predict an eruption is to watch each individual volcano and learn to recognize the warnings it gives before it erupts.

Scientists also collect measurements to give them information about volcanoes. They use seismographs to measure earth movements. This helps them to find out where volcanoes will erupt. As magma rises, it forces rocks apart which causes small earthquakes underground which can be detected on seismographs. This is an important measurement which allows scientists to tell exactly where the volcano will occur although not when it will explode.

A scientist, wearing a silvered asbestos suit to protect him, measures the flow of gas from a volcano.

EFFECTS OF VOLCANOES

Volcanoes are usually thought of as being dramatic and destructive. But they also bring benefits to people living in volcanic areas and do have some useful side-effects.

Hot springs

Hot springs occur in many parts of the world where underlying rocks allow water to penetrate deeply enough to be warmed by magma. Some hot springs naturally erupt as geysers and produce spectacular fountain displays.

The villagers on the island of Sao Miguel in the Azores use these springs to provide heat for cooking. They cook their food wrapped in cabbage leaves in holes dug in the ground, or in pots set in pools of boiling water, which have become yellow with the sulphur from the ground.

Springs also have other uses. In Japan, people bathe in hot springs for relaxation and as a health treatment – even outside in the winter when snow lies on the ground.

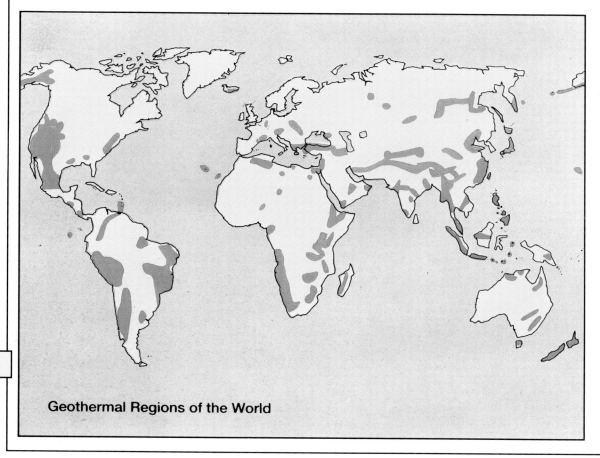

Geothermal Regions of the World

A map showing the areas of the world that use geothermal energy for heating or powering electricity generators.

Hot Water Underground

Porous rock

Aquifer

Heat from mantle

Non-porous rock

Hot spring

Geothermal energy

Deep under the ground are porous rocks, which hold water rather like a sponge does. Water collects in aquifers, which sit on hard, hot rocks and heat up the water above them. The hot water can be pumped to the surface by digging wells. This hot water is used to produce heat in the form of geothermal energy in some cold countries.

Above: Hot water collects in aquifers beneath the ground which can be pumped to the surface by digging wells.

Right: Sometimes hot water spurts naturally from hot underwater springs called geysers. This is Grand Geyser in Yellowstone National Park, USA.

Agriculture

The most widespread benefit of volcanoes is their affect on the agriculture of a region. When new lava covers an area, it is dull and lifeless, but old weathered lava produces very good soil. Old lava now makes soil fertile in Java, Indonesia, India, Sicily and the plains around Mount Etna in Italy. The lava contains many minerals needed by plants for strong, healthy growth. Good crops can be grown in areas with volcanic soil. Tenerife, one of the Canary Islands now grows grapes, tomatoes, potatoes and onions on what was once a desert of lava.

People who live on the Indonesian island of Bali use lava sand on their farms as a fertilizer.

The weather

The weather is often affected by volcanoes. Scientists believe that rocks, dust and ash blasted high into the atmosphere blocks out sunlight and makes the weather cooler.

When the Indonesian volcano of Tambori exploded in 1815 there was so little sunlight in Europe that the following year became known as the year without a summer. Spring lasted until an early autumn which quickly became winter. Harvests failed when frosts in June and July hit the farmlands across the continent and in many countries people starved.

Volcanoes produce more disasters than benefits. Many remain active from Alaska and Hawaii down to the South Seas, from Iceland to beyond the Mediterranean. Few remain asleep for ever.

Mount Ngauruhoe erupting in New Zealand. Some volcanoes blow a huge amount of rocks, dust and ash into the air which can affect the weather.

1. Build a model volcano

Picture the formation of a volcanic landscape. After a few eruptions from the vent, a small hill begins to grow and gets bigger and bigger as more layers of ash, lava and rocks are deposited. As we have seen, the shape of the volcano depends on the type of lava that comes out of it. Look at the pictures in this book and design and make a model of a volcanic landscape.

Materials:
Stiff card (50 cm x 50 cm)
Chicken wire mesh (75 cm x 75 cm)
Small plastic container
Wallpaper paste
Old newspapers
Waterproof paints
Bits of wood, and cocktail sticks
Old sponge
Glue

Method:

1. Ask an adult to crumple chicken wire to produce a mountainscape with a volcano crater.

Make sure the plastic container can fit in the top.

2. Mix the wallpaper paste, shred the newspaper and soak in paste for 5 minutes. Cover the wire with at least three layers of the papier mâché.

3. When it is thoroughly dry, paint and decorate the mountainscape. Add houses made of wood, and trees made of cocktail sticks and an old sponge.

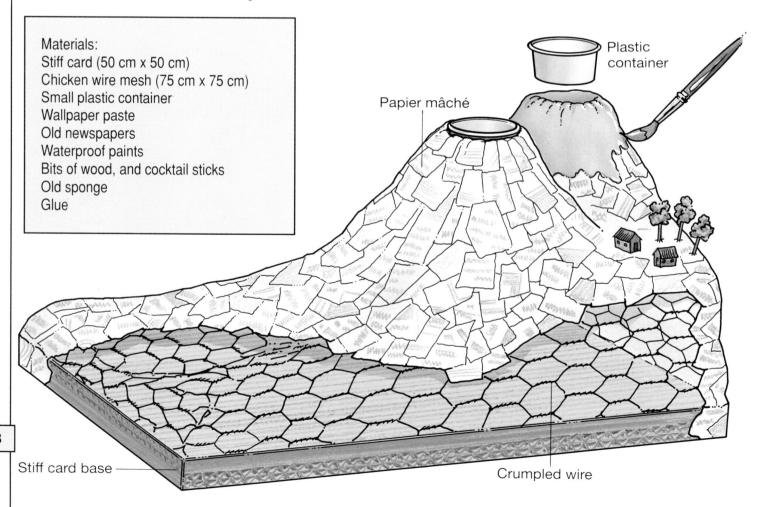

Plastic container

Papier mâché

Stiff card base

Crumpled wire

2. Bubbling lava

The funnel-shaped hollow at the top of the volcanic cone is called the crater. The bottom of the funnel opens into the pipe through which magma finds its way to the surface and flows down the sides. If you re-create this lava flow you will see the danger for people living in volcano areas, and why lava flows need to be blocked off by building dams in volcanic areas.

Materials:
Volcano model from project 1.
Baking soda (bicarbonate of soda)
Table vinegar (acetic acid)
Teaspoon
Modelling clay

Method:

1. Set the plastic container in the volcano crater of your model.

2. Place a single spoonful of bicarbonate of soda in the container and add the vinegar one spoonful at a time.

3. When your volcano starts to foam look and see where it flows. Try to build lava dams with modelling clay to direct the flow.

4. Clean your model with a damp sponge.

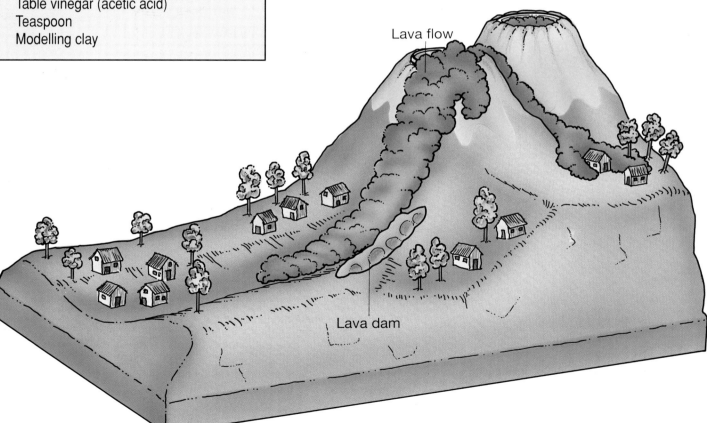

Lava flow

Lava dam

GLOSSARY

ARCHAEOLOGICAL To do with the study of ancient relics, particularly from pre-historic times.

CORE The centre and hottest part of the earth.

CRATER The depression, usually circular, caused by a volcanic eruption.

DORMANT Asleep. A volcano that has not erupted for many years is called dormant.

ERUPTION The forcing of lava and other volcanic material out of a weak spot in the earth's crust.

EVACUATE The organized movement of people out of a dangerous area.

EXCAVATION A search for archaeological or historic relics, usually by digging.

GEOTHERMAL To do with the heat from the inside of the earth.

GEYSER A spring that throws jets of hot water and steam into the air.

LANDSLIDE A fall of earth or rock, or both.

LAVA Liquid magma that erupts from a volcano and flows over the earth's surface.

MANTLE The layer of rock that lies between the earth's crust above and the core below.

MAGMA Molten rock produced inside the earth. When it flows out of the earth it is called lava.

MOSAIC Collection of stone or glass, making up a pattern.

PHOSPHOROUS A non-metallic element that glows in the dark.

PLATES The huge slabs of rock which make up the earth's crust.

POROUS Something that is able to absorb air or liquid.

REFUGEES People whose homes have been destroyed by warfare or natural disaster and who are forced to move to somewhere safer.

SEISMOGRAPH Instrument that registers the force and position of earth tremors.

SHOCK WAVES Energy spreading from underground tremors.

STRATA Layers of different rock.

TECTONIC To do with the movements of the earth's crust.

TREMORS Shaking of the earth at the ground surface caused by an earthquake.

TSUNAMI The Japanese name used to describe large sea waves caused by earthquakes or volcanic eruptions.

BOOKS TO READ

The Destruction of Pompeii
by Mike Rosen (Wayland, 1987)

The Eruption of Krakatoa
by Rupert Matthews (Wayland, 1988)

Volcanic Eruptions
by Jacqueline Dineen (Franklin Watts, 1991)

Volcano
by Brian Knapp (Macmillan, 1989)

Volcanoes
by Norman Barrett (Franklin Watts, 1989)

Volcanoes
by James Carson (Wayland, 1984)

Volcanoes and Earthquakes
by Martyn Bramwell (Franklin Watts, 1986)

Volcanoes and Earthquakes
by Terry Jennings (Oxford University Press, 1989)

Picture acknowledgements

The publishers would like to thank the following for allowing their photographs to be reproduced in this book: The Associated Press Ltd 20; Associated Press/Topham 5, 14; Bruce Coleman Ltd 16 below (Melinda Berge), 26 (Fritz Prenzel); John Frost's Historical Newspapers 4 (left); Geoscience Features Picture Library 18 (A. Lacroix), 22, 23 (Basil Booth); Frank Lane Picture Agency 4 right (USDA Forest Service), 7 (J.W Hughes, USDA); Oxford Scientific Films 12 (Hjalmar R. Bardarson), 25 (Michael Fogden); Photri 2/3 (B.Tippenreyter), 6/7, 11; Frank Spooner Pictures 19, 21; Tony Stone Worldwide 27; Werner Forman Archive 16/17; Zefa Picture Library *cover*.